Sustainable Living

Creating a Healthier Future for You and Your Family

By: Marcus McNeil

Table of Contents

Sustainable Living 101: What to Expect from Sustainability

It's hard to turn on the news or pick up a newspaper without reading stories about our planet in peril. Many years of industry and irresponsible management of Earth's resources have led to major issues with pollution, toxic waste, and climate change.

How can we combat what's happening to the globe? Sustainable living is the answer that many people are turning to in order to make the world a healthier place. But for many people, sustainable living seems like an unattainable lifestyle.

Before you become overwhelmed you should know that you can work toward sustainability in small steps. It might help to really understand what sustainable living means. In this chapter we'll look at an overview of sustainable living and help you to see the big picture.

In future chapters we'll look more in detail at specific aspects of sustainable living and what steps you can take to implement them into your lifestyle. Before you can decide what's right for you, it helps to know the basics.

A Philosophy for Life

Sustainable living is not a set of "rules" to follow. Rather it's a way of thinking that can help you to guide your life choices. Those who choose sustainable living are often concerned about a variety of issues including:

·   Environmental toxins

- Loss of natural resources
- Saving money
- Leaving a legacy for future generations
- Humane treatment of animals
- Pesticide-free food
- Eating whole foods and avoiding chemicals in food
- Keeping landfills to a minimum
- Fresh, clean drinking water
- Reducing dependency on corporate manufacturing
- Living with little negative impact on the environment

While it's difficult for one not to have any impact on the environment, sustainable living practices can help you to make sure you don't leave a bigger footprint than you want to leave for future generations.

There are any benefits to sustainable living that can be felt long before you leave the Earth to future generations. Your current health and happiness can be greatly affected by living these principles. There are many elements of this lifestyle that can apply to you.

Improved Health

People who practice sustainable living often have improved health from eliminating excess toxins and processed products from their lives. In Chapter 2 you'll learn more about how this can be the best choice for a long, healthy life.

Food Production

People who practice sustainable living often produce some or all of their own food. This component includes gardening and even maintaining livestock. Producing your own food guarantees that you know the quality of your meals.

In Chapters 3 and 4 you'll learn about producing your own food. Whether you want to have a small garden or a larger farm, you'll learn tips that fit your current situation and goals for lifestyle change.

Eliminating Waste

One of the key components of sustainable living is waste management. You'll want to completely use your resources and avoid the landfill. With sustainable living practices, you'll find that you can reuse many of your belongings, recycle them, and reduce your waste.

This includes your consumption of energy as well. You'll find that there are many simple steps that can help you to reduce your energy consumption and waste. We'll discuss these methods in Chapter 5.

Wise Use of Resources

It's also important that you use materials that are renewable. Sustainable living will focus on using materials that can be renewed. While some raw materials cannot be replaced once they've been used, there are many materials that are renewable and not limited.

Eliminating Harmful Chemicals

With sustainable living practices, you'll want to reduce the number of harmful chemicals that you use. While there are many products that are environmentally friendly, there are still quite a few products on the market that are not good for the planet – or for you.

When you choose to live sustainably, you'll almost always need to take a look at your chemical use and make a few changes. This can be done more easily than you might think without compromising cleanliness.

Making Sustainable Living Livable

Sustainable living is a philosophy that many people are adopting. As with anything, there are those who make extreme changes. You may be someone who wants to make a total lifestyle change and go full force.

However, many people find that they need to ease into a new lifestyle by making small, manageable choices. No matter what you desire, you can adapt sustainable lifestyle techniques to fit your lifestyle and your needs.

Beginning Your Journey

As you read through the chapters of this book, you may want to keep a pen and paper handy. Jot down the ideas that are the most appealing and fit your lifestyle best. Remember that you can make this lifestyle work for you at any level.

Why Choose a Sustainable Lifestyle: Improving the Planet's Health – and Yours

You may be wondering why someone would choose a sustainable lifestyle. It may seem like you have to go out of your way for these practices. But there are many reasons why it makes sense to choose sustainability.

Industry and Technology

Over the past 100 years or so, the world has undergone major changes that have been significant to the health of the planet. Technology has allowed us to do more at a faster pace. The industrial revolution and technology have led to many changes in the way we do things.

Most farms today are managed by using heavy machinery rather than the horse and plow that were used a hundred years ago. In fact, farming has moved away from the local family farm to a large corporate model.

Chemical fertilizers and pesticides are in high use and fossil fuels are used in large quantities to power the equipment that plants and harvests crops. Crops are monitored through technology such as GPS systems that monitor the harvest.

Additionally, many foods have been genetically modified to produce a higher yield or make them resistant to herbicides that control weeds. While some experts argue that this is not a problem for health or the environment, others disagree.

We have gotten so used to getting our food from supermarkets, that we take for granted how it gets there. It's important for the sustainability of the planet's resources that we pay attention to how products are made and transported.

Chemistry and Cleaning

While you may not remember a world where you didn't use chemicals to clean your home or your office that time once did exist. Many of the chemicals that are on the market now are good at filing your home with lovely scents, but they have a price to pay

Many of the everyday chemicals that are used to "clean" are actually quite harmful for the body and the planet. They leave behind toxins that can be harmful for people who suffer from asthma, allergies, and other respiratory problems.

Chemicals can also cause problems with skin. If your skin is very sensitive, you may find that many commercially available soaps and detergents can irritate you. Using products free of dyes and perfumes can help to alleviate the problem.

In addition, many chemicals can actually contribute to pollution of the environment. Sustainable living practices can actually reduce the amount of chemicals that end up in the water supply and in the ground. They can also help to alleviate you from symptoms caused by chemical use.

Financial Relief

While there may seem to be a little bit of out of pocket cost as you change your lifestyle, you'll find that sustainable living can actually save you a lot of money. Practices such as growing your own food and limiting waste can actually relieve your budget.

If you're looking for a way to pinch pennies, many of the sustainable living solutions for cleaning, managing energy waste, and repurposing objects could be the answer. You'll find that this type of life can help you to escape the trappings of materialism.

Peace of Consciousness

Many people choose sustainability because it brings peace of mind. You may be worried about the future of the planet for your children. You may be concerned about the ethical treatment of people and animals.

If you feel the ethical pull to make choices that will result in a healthier world, sustainable living might be for you. If you want to leave a legacy of ethical practices for your children and family, this is also a way toward your goals.

Leaving Excess Behind

Many people in society have the philosophy that more is more. It's difficult to live in the world and not constantly see things that you want or feel you have to have. We've become a planet where people are more concerned with what they have than what they can give.

If you're tired of keeping up with the Jones's and you're ready to live a simpler life, you're ready to move toward a sustainable lifestyle. This doesn't mean moving into a shack or living on a commune.

It seemly means that you'll learn to focus more on making sure your needs are met rather than collecting possessions. You'll be able to treasure what you have and not take it for granted as one does when they have too much.

Breathe Easier

When you contribute to the sustainability of the planet, you're literally improving the air quality. In this day and age there's more asthma and allergies than ever before. It's no surprise that the air quality is worse than it's ever been globally.

Planting trees, growing your own food, reducing your dependency on fossil fuels, and reducing your energy consumption can all contribute to a healthier atmosphere. Immediately you'll find you breathe a little easier and long-term, you can contribute to the reduction of global warming.

Sharing Your Example

Sometimes people worry that living sustainably as one person won't make much of an impact. But nothing could be further from the truth. When you choose sustainable living practices, you can actually begin a chain reaction.

When your neighbor sees you harvesting your garden he or she might decide it's time to start one, too. You might find that when riding your bicycle to work others see what you're doing and take their bike, too.

When you make one good choice, it will inevitably lead to more good choices. Your impact becomes much greater than what you alone did for the planet. Don't ever think that you alone can't make change happen. True change has to start with someone.

Changing Your Lifestyle

As you continue reading, you may feel like sustainable living requires you to change your life too much. Rest assured that as we talk about the big changes you can make, we'll also address small steps that will help you to sustain the Earth without having to change more than you're ready to change.

Getting Started with a Garden: Taking the First Steps toward Growing Your Own Food

Why Produce Your Own Food?

When there's a grocery store on every corner, it may seem like a foreign idea to produce your own food. But by growing your own food you can avoid some of the pitfalls that plague supermarket food.

Transportation Costs

Supermarket food is often transported many hundreds, if not thousands, of miles away from where it was grown. While it may allow you to have foods that aren't in season any time of year, this method of transporting food can be bad for the earth.

The amount of fossil fuels consumed to transport food around the globe is a major contributor to greenhouse emissions that many scientists propose lead to global warming. By lessening your dependence on supermarket produce, you'll also contribute to using less nonrenewable oil.

Chemicals

There are all kinds of chemicals used to produce food that you find in grocery stores. These chemicals are used to kill off pests, weeds, and to fertilize crops and increase the growth rate. There are also chemicals and waxes added to improve the look of the food so that it will be more appealing to consumers.

When you purchase produce, it's hard to tell exactly what was used in its manufacture unless it's labeled as organic. This produce is healthier, but it's not always affordable. In addition, the standards for being labeled "organic" may not meet your personal standards for sustainability.

By growing your own food you'll know exactly what type of soil, fertilizer, and types of plants you're growing. It will take the guesswork out of trying to choose healthy foods for your family.

Not only will you prevent your family from ingesting harmful chemicals, you'll also contribute to a healthier planet for now and for years to come. The fewer dangerous chemicals used for food production, the better.

Cost

Producing your own food can be cost effective. Given good soil, plenty of sun, and a little water most plants will grow and thrive. Seeds are inexpensive and seedlings can also be very affordable. A minimal investment can give you a great deal of produce.

Fun

While it may seem like a lot of work, growing your own food can be a very fun and satisfying experience. Checking your garden each day for signs of growth and to harvest your food can be very enjoyable.

If you're looking for a way to get your child to eat more fruits and vegetables, growing your own produce can be the perfect opportunity. Children are more likely to eat vegetables and fruits when they participated in the growing of them.

Lifelong Exercise

Growing a garden can also be a good form of physical activity for anyone. Even if your mobility is limited, there are gardens that can be grown to accommodate you. When you grow a garden you'll be getting a lot more physical activity than you might expect.

Getting Started with Growing

If you've decided you're ready to grow food in your own garden, you'll need to decide what method you'd like to use. A lot will depend on the space you have available and the climate in which you live.

Let's take a look at some of the options you may want to choose. Once you have an idea of what's required, you can decide what method is best for you. No matter what you choose, you'll be on the way to growing fresh, healthy food for you and your family.

Container Gardening

Container gardening is probably the simplest way to get started with gardening. It doesn't require a lot of space and it won't' require you to spend long hours tilling the ground and preparing soil.

With this method, you'll simply grow food in pots and other containers. This can be done even in the smallest spaces such as patios and porches. There are many foods that grow well in containers such as:

· Herbs

· Tomatoes

· Peppers

· Green beans

· Strawberries

· Onions

There are also many varieties of plants that have been specifically developed for growing in containers and can adapt very well. If you have limited space or you're just getting started with gardening, this may be the best choice for you.

You'll need very few supplies to get started including:

· Large planting containers

· Soil – make your own mix with compost, vermiculite, and peat

· Seeds

· Seedlings

· Cages for tomatoes and other plants that need to be supported

· Water hose or watering can

· Gloves

· Small gardening tools

You'll want to make sure that your containers are placed in the sunniest spot possible for most plants. If you don't have a sunny area, you may also want to consider purchasing grow lights. While they do take energy to operate, they can allow you to grow food when you otherwise could not.

Grow Boxes

Grow boxes provide a way to garden without using soil. This is called hydroponic growing and can be a good alternative if you'd like to have a great crop of plants without taking care of the soil conditions.

Grow boxes can be purchased commercially and used outside or indoors with a special grow light and careful climate control. If you've decided to use a grow box, you can grow just about anything as long as you make sure to follow the directions properly.

The downside to grow boxes is expense. Many people prefer to grow in the soil or containers they have rather than spending hundreds of dollars on grow boxes. However, if your budget can handle it, a grow box is a great way to grow your own food.

Gardening by the Foot

If you'd like to have a garden outside, but are very new at gardening, this technique can be very simple and successful. You'll need to set up a raised bed in your yard that measures four feet by four feet. Then you'll create a grid dividing it into 16 sections. See diagram below:

You'll need your container to be at least 6 inches deep and filled with soil. One way to prepare the ground below is to spread newspaper or weed control fabric that is sold at hardware stores. Then add your grid and fill with soil.

You can grow virtually any variety of plant with this method and it helps you to keep your plants organized. It's also easy to control weeds in this type of structure. You can build your own with wood, brick, or any other material that's non-toxic.

There are also commercially available kits for this type of container gardening. If you're not one to build things on your own, this might be a good alternative. You can find many books and websites that contain specific information about this type of gardening.

Square foot gardening is a great way to get started with gardening if you want to do more than a container garden, but you don't have the space or soil for a traditional row garden.

Traditional Row Gardening

Traditional gardening is another way that you can grow your own food. For this type of garden you'll need a piece of land that gets plenty of sun. You'll need to till the area that you want to use for your garden to help loosen the soil.

You'll also need to add organic material to the soil. This process is called amending the soil. You can do this by adding compost, peat, and manure to your soil. It's easiest to add these materials with the tiller so that you can get them all mixed appropriately.

With traditional row gardening, you'll need to have more space and it will require that you have more heavy-duty tools. However, the benefit of this type of garden is the ability to grow a lot of food for your family.

Determining What to Plant

When it comes to gardening, it's critical that you plan ahead and know what will grow best in your space. There are a few considerations you need to make when deciding what you're going to plant.

Climate

First and foremost, you need to take a look at the climate in which you live. In the United States, the country has been divided into growing zones. This can help you to determine what zone you're in and what you can grow.

Conveniently, seed packets and plants typically list on the package the zones in which they grow as well as the time period in which you should plant. You'll want to make sure to stick to the planting schedule listed.
However, you'll also want to speak with other local growers to make sure that there aren't extenuating circumstances. For example, a particularly long winter can delay the time for planting in the spring.

It's best to get advice from other people in your area about what will grow well and determining the best time to plant. While books and packages can give you guidelines, tried and true experience will be a better determination of what and when to plant.

Soil

The type of soil you have will also determine what will grow well in your area. If you're not sure what type of soil you have, you can usually head to the local nursery with a soil sample. There it will be analyzed.

Once soil is analyzed, you'll receive information about what needs to be added to the soil in order for plants to grow. Sometimes soil is already for growing, but in many cases you'll need to add organic material in order to restore nutrients needed for gardening.

Sunlight

Many vegetables need full sunlight in order to grow. However, some can grow in partial sun. You'll need to make sure that you have a place for your garden that receives a great deal of sunlight.

If you're unable to grow in full sun, you'll need to look for plants that will grow with fewer hours of sun exposure. This can be a difficult, though not impossible task. In order to grow plants such as tomatoes and squashes you will need full sun.

Gather Resources

Before getting started with your garden, it's a good idea to gather as many resources as possible. There are many great books about gardening and you can even find books about gardening in your particular region.

In addition, you can find online resources that include message boards where gardeners share tips and tricks as well as ask questions. This can be one of the most helpful resources if you're having a dilemma you can't solve from a book.

You may also have a local resource from the agriculture extension in your area. These are agencies in most counties that can provide information on gardening and help you to learn more about the growing season in your area.

Consider taking classes on gardening as well. There's nothing like getting direct instruction and literally getting your hands dirty. Classes can be found at local nurseries as well as local botanical gardens sponsored by cities.

Finally, talk to as many people as you can who garden. Create a network of people who know what they're doing and can help you with specific questions and concerns. You may even be able to set up an exchange with friends.

For example, if you choose to plant tomatoes and your friend plants squash, you can divide the harvest so that you each have what you need without having to grow different types of plants. This is also a great way to exchange if you don't have space to grow all that you would like.

Your Tastes

Don't forget to think about what you like when you're deciding what to plant. For example, if you know you just hate squash, don't spend a lot of time trying to plant and nurture squash plants.

You may want to try new things as well. You may find that things you didn't like before taste so much better when they're freshly picked from your own yard. However, while you're experimenting with new flavors, you'll want to plant small amounts.

Eliminating Chemicals

While you're working on changing your lifestyle to one that practices sustainable living, you'll want to make sure you do all you can to eliminate harmful chemicals from your garden. This is easier to do now than it was a few years ago because many companies have responded to the desire of people to grow organically.

Pest Control

If your garden is plagued with pests, there are several things you can do before resorting to poisons that will not only get rid of unwanted critters but can also poison your food supply. Rest assured you can have a pest-free garden without having to add poisons.

First, you should know that there are many things you can plant that will actually deter predators from your garden. For example, planting marigolds in your garden will repel many bugs. Check with your local nursery to find out what plants can repel the pests you have in your yard.

Barriers can also be created to prevent rodents from getting into your garden. Chicken wire with small holes can be added around your garden area to keep rabbits out. You can create much taller "cages" around your plants to keep squirrels out.

In addition, electric fences can be used to help prevent unwanted guests. Most of these are designed to surprise critters without harming them. While this may be a last resort, it could be deemed necessary if you have extreme problems with squirrels.

If you have infestations of grub worms or insects, you may want to consider organic pest control. For example, BT (bacillus thuringiensis) is a type of bacteria that can be purchased in sprays or powders.

This bacteria kills off insects but is not harmful to humans and is naturally occurring in the environment. It's a natural way to eliminate insect problems from your garden. There are many commercially available formulas for ridding your garden of pests without causing harm.

Natural predators can also be used to help get rid of unwanted pests. For example, adding ladybugs to your garden will help to eliminate aphids from attacking plants. Having a pet dog or cat can also help get rid of unwanted rodents.

Not all invaders to your garden should be considered unwelcome. You actually need insects to help pollinate plants and decompose the soil. Earthworms are excellent at helping to decompose organic matter in the soil and provide nutrients for plant growth.

In general, unless insects are eating your plants leaves and harvesting your veggies before you get the chance, you may just want to leave them alone. Part of living a sustainable lifestyle is learning which organisms can actually work with you for plant growth.

Fertilization

While there are many chemical fertilizers on the market, you'll find that they are unnecessary and that there are many organic products that will do as good of a job without adding harm. There are several options.

First, manure does an excellent job of restoring nutrients to your soil. You can purchase manure at many nurseries. If you live in a rural area you may want to speak to a local farmer and see if you can get manure at a discount – or even free.

Composting is another excellent source of fertilization for your soil. You can purchase compost commercially or you can create your own compost pile. Making your own will allow you to recycle some wastes and use them for a purpose.

Compost is actually a mixture of organic materials that are broken down and then can be used in soil as fertilizer. The finished compost will be rich in color and will be an incredible addition to your garden.

How do you make a compost pile? It's actually quite simple. You'll needs to start with some sort of container. Many people make their own using plywood – you can even use wooden pallets tied together. You'll just need a large container – at least 4 feet by 4 feet.

Your container needs to have holes for aeration and it needs to be accessible for turning the materials inside. You can also purchase commercial containers that are specifically designed for composting.

Next you'll need to collect materials that are appropriate. Some examples of materials are:

- Dried leaves
- Vegetable scraps
- Fruit scraps
- Spoiled fruits and vegetables
- Eggshells
- Coffee grounds
- Dead plant material

You'll want to avoid any type of animal products such as meat or milk. These will cause your compost to develop harmful bacteria. Once you combine materials, you'll need to add water. Your compost pile should always be a little damp.

In addition, you'll need to turn the compost as often as possible. The more often you turn it, the faster materials will decompose. It's a good idea to turn it daily if you want compost to develop within a few weeks.

You'll want to make sure to keep a bucket in your home to collect ingredients for the compost pile. This is a living process that you can add to all the time. Every time you add materials to your compost, make sure you turn it.

Compost piles will naturally have a lot of warmth because of the biological processes occurring inside. If you're having trouble getting your compost to break down, you may want to try adding some existing compost to get the good bacteria started.

Rotating your crops can also help keep the soil you're using fertilized. There are many plants that complement each other. For example, planting peas and carrots near one another will help them both to thrive.

Make sure not to plant the same crop in the same spot every time. Look for guides on crop rotation to make sure you're getting the most out of the process. This is one of the oldest and simplest forms of sustaining the land.

Not Ready for Gardening?

You may be interested in sustainable living, but feel like now is not the time for starting your own garden. If you don't have space, the climate, or the time to garden there are still many thing you can do to contribute to the health of the planet as well as your own.

Buy Local

The less your food has to travel, the fewer fossil fuels will be used for your food. When you can, try to buy produce from local farmers or farmers markets. Not only will you be supporting local business, you'll also find that the produce tastes delicious and fresh.

Farmer's markets have sprung up in many urban areas. If you don't live near farmers, check to see if farmers are coming to your area to sell their harvest. It's also possible to find local produce at your local supermarket.

Many supermarkets carry produce from local farmers. You'll simply need to look for labels in the produce section for local produce. This is a great way to support your local farmer without having to look further than your own neighborhood.

Buy Organic

Organic products also offer a sustainable solution for families. These products are often more expensive than their non-organic counterparts. You'll want to look for the USDA symbol for organic produce to guarantee you're buying organic.

While this can cut down on the dangers of the food you buy, it's important to know that things that are labeled organic aren't always regulated as well as one would like. You're still better off being able to purchase from someone local whom you can trust.

Organic foods also tend to travel great distances to get to the supermarket. That means your food requires the use of fossil fuels. But when you're not able to buy locally, organic is the next best choice.

Join a Co-Op

Another option that's gaining popularity is a farm co-op. To participate, you typically will buy a share of the harvest. You might have to pay up front or through monthly payments. Purchasing a share will allow you to get a percentage of the harvest.

This type of plan will result in getting a box of varied produce from a farm. The vegetables and fruits you receive will be those in season and ready to harvest each month. This is a great way to buy local regularly.

Some co-ops also require volunteer work where you and/or your family come to the farm and actually help to take care of and harvest the crops. While you don't have to do all the gardening yourself, this gives you a chance to participate in the growth of your food.

It's really the best of both worlds to help nurture and care for the food you eat without the burden of having to be 100% responsible for your crops. Many people find that this is a great way to get delicious produce at a good price and help their family get involved in food production.

The Intimacy of Food

It's so common that we don't think too much about the food we eat. But really, food is the most intimate relationship one has in life. You share your body with food several times each day.

You'll want to make sure that what you're eating is something that's safe and contributes to a sustainable system for the planet. We've spent a lot of time talking about adding produce to your diet, but what about animal protein? In the next chapter we'll tackle sustainable livestock.

From Chickens to Cows: Taking Care of Livestock in Your Backyard

For many people, a vegetarian diet is not desirable. If you're a vegetarian or a vegan, you'll probably want to skip this chapter. But if you enjoy eating animal products such as meat, milk, and eggs this chapter is for you.

Problems with Livestock

One of the growing problems with the environment is that animal products aren't grown and harvested in a way that's healthy for the environment or healthy for the people consuming them. In fact, when you know what's going on with this industry, you may find yourself in shock.

Ethical Treatment of Animals

For many people, raising their own livestock is about making sure that the animals they depend on for food are treated with respect. That means living a life that is natural for them until they are harvested.

It also means making sure that when they're harvested, it's done in the most humane way possible. Some vegetarians believe that there's no way to eat animals in a humane way, but for those who choose to eat animals there can be ethical practices.

Making sure animals have plenty of space to move around is critical to their health. They also need to be fed the proper diet and be free from abuse. In many major meat packing facilities and poultry houses, this simply isn't the case.

Treating animals in an ethical manner also produces a healthier harvest. For example, cows that are fed on a diet of corn have a higher amount of E. coli bacteria in their systems leading to food safety problems. Those fed on a diet of grass shed most of that dangerous bacteria.

Not only will cows have fewer problems with bacteria, they'll also have a lower amount of fat. Chickens fed a natural diet and allowed to move produce eggs with lower levels of cholesterol and saturated fat.

Antibiotics and Hormones

Animals raised in close quarters like chicken houses and feedlots have more risk of infection. As a result, many are treated with antibiotics. What they eat gets transferred to the consumer. That means that people are being exposed to high levels of antibiotics unnecessarily.

This can lead to being drug resistant. That means that more and more bacteria are becoming resistant to the antibiotics that are used to treat infection. More and more people are finding that their infections have to be fought with stronger drugs to counteract some of these effects.

Hormones are also often added to animals in order to make them grow larger and faster and produce a bigger harvest. Eating hormones in food can lead to problems with your body's own hormones.

Unsafe Food Handling

There have been many problems with bacterial outbreaks as a result of the way animal products are handled. Because of poor conditions in feedlots, chicken houses, and meat processing plants the safety of your food is often at risk.

The bacteria levels in food purchased from the supermarket far surpasses levels found in food that is grown in a sustainable way. When you're in charge of the processing of your own food, you can limit the problems with infection.

Environmental Problems

Modern animal use has also caused problems with the environment. Animal consumption is at its highest rate worldwide. Emissions from cattle including pigs and cows – methane gas from digestion – are considered a major threat to the climate of the globe.

In addition, the wastes from these animals are not always disposed of properly. This causes problems with contaminating the environment around large feedlots for pigs and cattle. Raising your own cattle helps to limit these effects.

Poor Working Conditions for People

The meat industry is one of the most dangerous industries for workers. The working conditions are often not safe for the people who raise, slaughter, and butcher the animals. Large corporations often take advantage of people who are unskilled workers and illegal immigrants.

Raising Your Own Animals

Because of the danger of commercial farming as well as its effects on the environment, many people are turning to raising and harvesting their own animals. While you may not be ready to move to a rural area where you can have livestock, you may be surprised how much you can do right now.

Chickens

One of the easiest animals to begin with is the chicken. In fact, raising chickens has become so popular that many cities are now allowing chickens to be raised inside the city limits. It's easy to set up a chicken coop for one or two chickens.

Before you get started, you need to check with your local laws to make sure you are legally able to raise chickens. While many urban areas don't allow livestock, chickens are frequently allowed.

The benefits of raising chickens include having fresh eggs delivered right to your backyard. You may also choose to raise chickens for their meat. Chickens are relatively easy to dress and inexpensive to raise.

To get started, you'll need to decide on housing. Chicken coops can be designed with very simple materials such as wood and chicken wire. You'll want to make sure that your chickens have plenty of space in which to move around.

You'll also need to find a supplier for your chicks. Check with local feed stores to find a supplier. You may also want to look online for suppliers. You'll need to determine which type of chicken you want to purchase as well.

It's a good idea to gather as many resources as possible and speak with others who have raised chickens to make sure you understand the ins and outs of this endeavor. You'll find that people who've also raised chickens will be great at answering questions and giving you tips.

Goats

Goats are lively animals that are fairly easy to raise. They are smaller than many other livestock animals and you can get great benefits from them in the form of goat's milk. This type of milk is very healthy and versatile.

Make sure first that your local laws support the raising of goats. Then you'll need to make sure you have the proper shelter and food for your goat. Goats are notorious for mischief, so you'll need to make sure you have an area that's "goat proof".

Before investing your time and energy into goat raising, you'll need to gather resources and get prepared. You may want to talk to your local agriculture extension to get help with making preparations.

Cows and Pigs

Cows and pigs are a substantially greater undertaking than chickens and goats. In addition, most urban areas have laws preventing citizens from raising large animals such as these. Before you can raise these animals, you'll need to make sure your area is zoned for livestock and that you have adequate space.

Most likely, you'll need to live in a rural area with a great deal of land in order to raise large animals. It's important that you gather resources, investigate the costs, and plan ahead before jumping into raising livestock of this size.

If you're able to raise these large animals, you'll find that there are many benefits. You'll be able to eat meat that's free of hormones and antibiotics. You can also ensure that your animals live a life that's free from stress and in appropriate conditions.

Cows provide fresh milk you can use to make all kinds of dairy products including your own cheese and butter. Fresh milk that's unpasteurized also has great health benefits. In addition, you can harvest livestock for beef.

Raising your own pigs will allow you to have a large variety of pork products that are free from artificial hormones. You can make your own sausages, bacons, hams, and know you'll be eating quality food. In addition, pigs are actually less difficult to raise than cows.

When it comes to processing your meat, some people choose to slaughter and butcher their own animals. However, many people opt to take their animals to a meat processor to be slaughtered and butchered. This actually can help to support small business in your community.

Other Animals

There are many other animals you may consider raising as part of the choice to live sustainably. Here are a few you might want to consider for their meat as well as other benefits:

- rabbits – meat and fur
- sheep – wool and meat
- honey bees – pollination for the garden and honey
- guineas – insect control
- Ducks – meat and feathers
- Geese – meat and feathers
- Turkeys – meat
- Pheasants – meat

Every animal will have its own needs for shelter, food, and habitat. Make sure that you research each one individually before making the decision to purchase and raise them. You'll also need to be prepared to harvest the meat.

A Changing Mindset

If you grew up in an urban area where animals were often pets – not food – you may have to change to a new way of thinking. Raising animals in your backyard for food won't work if you become too emotionally attached to them.

People who are raised on farms where animals are routinely harvested for meat tend to look at animals in a different way. You may want to practice a few of these tips to prevent the emotional connection with your farm animals:

- Don't name farm animals.
- Don't allow them to enter your home.

· Make sure to educate your children about the purpose of animals

While it's important to remember the purpose of raising animals, it's also important to make sure they are treated with respect. Not becoming emotionally attached is not the same as becoming abusive. You must still care for all of the needs of your farm animals.

Not Ready to Raise Animals for Food?

For many people raising their own livestock is essential to their sustainable living practices. But for others, especially in urban areas, it may not be possible to do so. Even if you're able to raise the animals, it may not be something that you want to do.

If you're not ready to make the big commitment to raise your own animals, there are several things you can do to contribute to sustainability of the planet as well as improve your own physical health.

Buy Local

You may find that within an hour or two of where you live there are farmers that sell their animal harvests. In fact, this is becoming more and more common as people understand their responsibility to the planet as well as the dangers of commercial livestock.

A quick online search may help you to find someone in your area. He or she will be able to send you information when products are ready to be purchased, picked up, or delivered. There's something very reassuring about going to a farm and buying your food.

You'll be able to meet the farmer who helped to raise the animals, see how the animals are living, and have peace of mind that you're buying a quality product. You'll want to ask about the animal's diet and even ask for a tour of the farm.

Farmer's markets provide another opportunity to buy locally grown food. Many farmers set up stands to sell their meat or to take orders for it and arrange delivery times. This is another great way to contribute to sustainable agriculture.

You may find that by purchasing whole or part of an animal you'll also be able to save quite a bit of money. Investing in a freezer can help your meat to last 6 months or more depending on the product.

Buy Organic

If farmer's markets aren't available to you, you may want to make the decision to purchase organic meats. Most supermarkets now carry meats that are grown organically and are free from hormones.

You can also purchase milk that's harvested from cows fed an organic diet or from small farms instead of large commercial farms. Eggs, cheese, and other dairy products can also be purchased this way.

Eat Less Meat

You don't have to become a vegetarian to help reduce the environmental impact of meat production. Simply skipping meat one day a week can help to reduce the effects of global warming.

If you want to live more sustainably, a simple step is to eat fewer meals with meat. Even limiting meat consumption by one or two days can have a big impact on your carbon footprint. This comes from reduced emissions by animals as well as emissions from transporting meat across the country.

Simple Steps to a Healthier World

While sustainable living can be something that requires a lot of work, it can also be done simply. If you're not ready to leave city life and move to the country to run your own small farm, you can make some small choices that will have big effects.

If you're ready to start raising your own animals, don't try to start all at once. Try raising something easy such as chickens first. Once you have the hang of it, you can graduate to more demanding animals.

If you know you're never going to want to raise your own animals, don't feel bad. You can still support sustainable living practices by limiting your consumption of meat, buying organic, or buying from local farms.

Even taking one simple step to reduce the harmful effects of commercial meat production can have a big impact. You'll also be setting a great example for your friends, family, and community.

While being a vegan (consuming no animal products) is certainly a viable option, you don't have to give meat and animal products up completely in order to contribute to a healthy planet. You'll also find that when you eat meat grown in an ethical and healthy way, your own health will improve.

Waste Not Want Not: Producing and Conserving Energy in Your Home

A huge part of sustainable living is controlling the amount of energy you consume. It helps to understand where energy comes from so that you understand why it's so critical to conserve it. In this chapter we'll look at the forms of energy we use as well as how you can reduce your consumption of planet polluting energy and increase the amount of clean energy you use.

Energy Sources

There are many ways in which we get energy all over the planet. Some of them are more sustainable than others. It's virtually impossible to use no energy, but there are certainly better choices as well as ways to reduce your consumption.

Fossil Fuels

A great deal of our energy comes from fossil fuels. We use them in the form of gasoline to drive our cars and other mechanics. Fossil fuels are also used to power generators to produce electricity. Over half of our electricity comes from burning coal.

Fossil fuels are those sources of energy that come from organic materials buried deep beneath Earth's surface. They can be liquid, solid, or gas. Liquid and gas fossil fuels come from dead animal remains that have broken down over long periods of time.

These include oil and natural gas. These fossil fuels are obtained by using large drills.

These can be dangerous and environmentally toxic. There have been several environmental catastrophes involving the drilling and transport of oil.

Coal, a solid fossil fuel, comes from the dead remains of plants that have petrified over millions of years. It is mined from deep within the ground. Mining is one of the most dangerous professions in the world as workers can become trapped underground.

The use of fossil fuels greatly contributes to air pollution. As the fuel is burned, it emits carbon dioxide and other chemicals into the atmosphere. Fossil fuels are considered nonrenewable resources. Once they have been used up, they can't be replaced. As a society we are heavily dependent on these resources.

Solar Energy

The sun is the ultimate source of energy that powers the earth. It provides so much energy that people have spent many years working to harness that power and convert it into electricity that can be used easily.

There are a few ways that the sun's energy can be used in modern times. One is passive solar energy. This is when structures are built to take advantage of the natural benefits of warmth from the sun.

Active solar energy uses photovoltaic cells to capture the sun's energy. They can be used to power small electronics such as the ever popular solar calculator. But they can also be used to power larger systems and are sometimes used in homes to supplement traditional electricity.

Solar energy doesn't leave any pollutants behind, making it a clean source of energy that promotes a sustainable environment. And while it has many benefits, it's not without drawbacks.

While solar energy is considered renewable – using the sun's energy doesn't take away from the energy it produces – but it is expensive. The equipment to harness solar energy can be very pricey. It's also bulky as it takes a great deal of surface area to capture the sun's rays.

Wind Energy

Capturing the energy from the wind is nothing new. People have used windmills for hundreds of years to turn turbines that power machinery. Now those turbines are being used to generate electricity.

Wind energy is renewable - using the wind doesn't take away from it. It's also nonpolluting. However, the equipment required to harness the wind in an effective manner is very costly and large.

Wind farms are cropping up in areas where there is a lot of access to wind energy. This tends to be in large, flat areas. Recently coastlines have been the favorite site of wind farm developers because of the access to moving air.

Some of the major complaints about wind farms are that they can be loud and unsightly. It usually takes hundreds of windmills facing different directions to actually capture enough energy to use for a power source.

In rare instances, people have purchased windmills for personal use. While the initial cost is great, they tend to pay for themselves over their lifetime in saved energy costs. Wind energy is also sustainable in that it doesn't pollute the air.

Some commercial electric companies get their energy from windmill use. This isn't accessible to everyone and the rates tend to be a little higher. However, people who can access it often appreciate knowing they are using sustainable energy.

Water Energy

Just as windmills use wind energy to turn turbines, water can also be harnessed to generate electricity. This is most obviously seen in areas where there are large dams such as the Hoover Dam in Nevada.

While this type of energy is renewable, some environmentalists disagree with the practice of damming up rivers and rerouting water unnaturally. To combat some of the problems that occur from changing the natural ecosystem, there are usually measures put into place.

For example, many dams have nearby hatcheries to help sustain the native populations of fish in the area. However, some changes to the environment such as water temperature changes make it impossible to keep the ecosystem intact as it was before.

Nuclear Power

Nuclear power is a source of energy that tends to be quite controversial. It seems like just about every 20 years or so there's an event at a nuclear power plant that causes people to question its safety.

Most recently, the disaster at the nuclear plant in Japan has people considering the use of nuclear energy. Concerns about radiation exposure for workers and nearby citizens make nuclear power difficult to sell.

There's also concern regarding the wastes that nuclear power plants produce. Waste from these plants can stay radioactive for many, many years. Storing it safely and effectively is another issue.

Bio-Fuels

Many living organisms produce energy that can be harnessed as fuel. There are several ways this can be done. Burning wood, for example, is a type of bio-fuel. Burning trash is another way the energy can be released.

In recent years, scientists are working to find ways to convert biological organisms into fuel. Corn and soy are the most common plants involved in this research. Algae is also another avenue for energy that's being explored.

Some vehicles are actually being converted to run on vegetable oils. These burn much cleaner than cars running on fossil fuels. However, you can't buy this type of car at a car dealership. Instead, it will have to be retrofitted by someone who knows how to do it.

It's thought that biofuels hold the key to the energy and global warming crisis. However, ecologists worry that this will make it more difficult to manage the food supply globally. It's a catch 22 situation that can't be resolved immediately.

Reducing Dependence on Energy in Your Home

Because there aren't any easy answers for using fuels that are clean and have little impact on the environment, the best way to embrace sustainable living at this time is to reduce your dependency on energy. Then when you do need electricity or fuel, you can make smarter choices.

There are several choices you can make that will allow you to live in the modern world and still reduce your global impact. The first step is becoming aware of the energy that you use and analyzing what changes you can make.

Lighting

One of the greatest energy drains on the planet is keeping things bathed in light. Everywhere you go there are artificial lights that run 24 hours a day. While it's great to be able to function at all hours, this definitely takes its toll on the environment.

When it comes to your home or your office, you can do a few easy things to make sure that you're not wasting more energy than you need. First, turn off lights you don't need. This seems obvious, but when you begin to take notice you may find that you're using lights unnecessarily.

Make sure that when you leave a room, you turn off the lights. You may even want to invest in motion sensor lights that are programmed to turn on and off when you enter and leave a room. This makes it easier for you to save energy without having to think too much about it.

The type of bulb you use can also make a big difference in your energy consumption. Incandescent bulbs are the kind of bulbs we all grew up using. However, they use a lot of energy and much of that is lost as heat.

Fluorescent lighting is much more energy efficient. Manufacturers have been working on ways to make look more aesthetically pleasing and produce a warmer light. While these lights cost more up front, they last a long time and use much less energy.

During the day, make use of natural light so that you don't need to use overhead lighting and lamps. Keep your blinds and shades open and make use of the windows in your home. Before you leave your home, make sure you turn off extra lights that aren't in use.

Electronics

It's a world full of electronics from televisions to computers to iPods. There's no way to turn back time and become less dependent on this equipment for work and for your home life. However, you can make some smart decisions to minimize your carbon footprint.

Set computers and tablets to energy saver modes. This will allow your monitor to turn off when you're not really using the computer. You should also turn off or hibernate machines when they're not going to be in use for long periods of time.

When you leave the office for the weekend, turn off the computer. Many people leave computers running all the time and this drains energy unnecessarily. This can be true in homes as well.

Unplug cords when they aren't in use. While you may not be using the energy that travels through the cord, they can still drain energy. Don't leave items plugged in if you're not using them – even items such as hair dryers, toasters, and microwaves use energy when they're not being used.

When you buy large appliances, look for items that have energy star ratings. These items use less energy to do their job. Not only will this save energy, it can also save you quite a bit of money on your utility bills. In addition, there are some tax breaks for purchasing items that have this rating.

Heating and Cooling

Most of your monthly energy bill probably comes from heating and cooling your home. Some people who embrace sustainable living choose not to use air conditioning and heating. However, you don't have to let go of these comforts completely in order to practice sustainability.

In the summer, keep your thermostat set to a higher temperature than you would normally prefer. While some people like to keep it set at 72 degrees, you'll find that 78 is still a relief from the heat but uses less energy.

Here are a few tips for staying comfortable in the summer without being an energy hog:

· Keep blinds and curtains closed during the part of the day when windows are being exposed to strong sun.

·   Use ceiling fans and oscillating fans when you are in a room – make sure to turn them off when you leave.

·   Dress in light clothing.

·   Limit the use of your oven during hot parts of the day – cook outside, use the stovetop, crockpot, or eat cool dishes.

·   Use lighter linens for bedding.

In the winter, you can also lower your thermostat to 68 degrees to save some energy. You'll find that this temperature can be quite comfortable if you find other ways to bundle up. There are several things you can do in winter to stay warm:

·   Use thermal curtains on windows that help to trap heat and keep you warm.

·   Add flannel sheets and down comforters to your beds to stay warm at night.

·   Wear slippers on your feet.

·   Add insulation film to windows to lose less heat.

·   Block drafts with weather stripping.

·   Place a rolled up towel across the threshold of doors to prevent drafts.

Windows

Many people lose huge amounts of energy through old windows. One way you can help to save energy is to replace old windows with new double-pane insulated windows. This will help to trap the energy in your home.

While new windows can be a pricey update to your home, over time they'll pay for themselves in energy costs. Many companies offer these window updates. You'll want

47

to get several estimates and check references before hiring someone to do this work.

Utility Companies

Many areas have utility companies that get their energy from green sources such as wind energy. Research your area and look for companies that offer energy that's also sustainable. It may cost a bit more, but it will be more sustainable.

Home Design

If you're in the market for a new home, you should consider sustainable planning. Choosing the direction in which your home faces, the types of landscaping that you put in place, as well as the placement of windows can make a big impact on energy use.

Make sure that the home you're building is as efficient as possible with insulated windows, insulated walls, and energy efficient heating and cooling systems. You may also want to consider adding solar panels to supplement other energy use.

Ask the Experts

Just about every home has areas where energy is wasted. It's a good idea to have professionals come and inspect your house to determine where energy is being lost. Many companies have popped up in urban areas to help with this process.

A consultant will inspect your home and find out where you have problems with insulation. They'll also make suggestions for ways you can limit your energy use. This is helpful for determining the specific needs of your family and your home.

Reducing Transportation Energy

Another huge demand on energy is transportation. People need to get from place to place, but the way you do it can make a big difference in your carbon footprint. You don't have to stay home all day to help the environment. Some simple changes can make a big impact.

No Waste Walking

One of the best ways to save on energy use is to go where you need to go by foot. While many people live too far away from work or school to walk, an urban area usually presents itself with many opportunities to walk.

If you live within a few blocks of the grocery store, try walking to pick up items instead of driving. Many people drive to every destination – even if it's a block or two away. Walking can be a great way to save energy.

Many communities have developed walking school buses where adults supervise large groups of children walking to school. It helps if you have a pedestrian-friendly neighborhood with sidewalks, crosswalks, and traffic lights programmed for walking.

Peddle Your Way

When you're traveling to places that are close by, you might want to consider dusting off your bicycle and riding to your destination. Not only will you reduce your dependence on fossil fuels, you'll also get your body in better shape.

Carpool

If you know several people who are going the same place at the same time, a carpool can help save energy and money. For a carpool, you can take turns with other people driving to work or school.

Carpooling can be a great way to travel. You'll need to set up a regular schedule or rotation for drivers. You could each have a day of the week that you drive or you could rotate on a weekly basis.

If only one person has a large enough vehicle for a crowd, you could simply ask for money for gas as well as wear and tear on your vehicle. This will save everyone money on fuel as well as help reduce your dependence on fossil fuels and reduce the emissions into the atmosphere.

Public Transportation

If you live in an area with public transportation, take advantage of it. In many cities public transportation is an effective way to get from place to place. It's inexpensive and it allows you to relax on your daily commute.

Subways and trains are particularly nice because they offer the added benefit of avoiding commuter traffic. Public transportation also costs less than driving oneself from place to place. Check with your local transit office for monthly passes that give a deeper discount.

In many urban areas, public transportation costs are even lower during summer months when the air quality can be lower. You may also find that many companies get discounts for employees who want passes for public transit.

Efficient Vehicles

Cars are becoming more and more fuel efficient. If you're in the market for a new vehicle, make sure to choose one that meets the needs of your family and is also fuel efficient. Hybrid vehicles run on a combination of fuel and electricity.

There are also vehicles that run on flex fuel or natural gas that burn cleaner and get better mileage. These vehicles tend to be more expensive than older model cars, so you'll need to balance your financial needs with sustainable living practices.

Saving Energy for the Future

While you may live in a modern world, there are many ways you can tailor a modern existence that uses less energy. You don't have to give up your internet connection or your comfortable environment to reduce your carbon footprint.

Making simple changes can help you go from being an energy guzzler to an energy saver. You'll find that taking small steps makes the process less overwhelming than trying to change everything at once.

Once you get comfortable and a new behavior becomes a habit, you can add a new step. Getting your entire family on board can also make it easier. When you all have the same focus, it makes it easier to make changes.

Reduce, Reuse, Recycle: Sustaining the Earth by Managing Waste

One of the biggest problems that the Earth faces is consumption and disposability. In the modern world we are more likely to throw something away and replace it than we are to repurpose it or repair it.

A principle of sustainable living is that we use up what we have, recycle what we don't need anymore, and repurpose things that can serve a new purpose. Another principle is not taking more than you need.

Reduce

Do you have more than you need? If you're like most people you do. People tend to have closets full of clothes they never wear – or wore once. They tend to have garages full of equipment that isn't used. And you may have entire rooms dedicated to storage.

If you have to have a storage unit to contain your belongings, you probably have more than you need. There are several things you can do to minimize over-consumption. This doesn't mean you can never buy anything – just that you're thoughtful.

Why does it matter how much stuff you have? Well, when you buy items produced in a factory they often require the use of nonrenewable energy sources. Having more items also means you have to have more space.

The more space you have the more energy it takes to heat and cool it. Buying a lot of stuff also means that you probably dispose of more items. To keep the landfills from overflowing, you can start by buying less.

Here are a few tips for consuming less:

- Before making clothing purchases make sure you buy items that can be worn more than once with more than one outfit.
- Buy clothes made of sustainable fabrics.
- When you purchase items, consider buying gently use items. You'll save things from the landfill – and you'll save money.
- When going shopping, make a list and stick to it.
- Purchase items that serve more than one purpose – this allows you to buy fewer items.
- Before buying anything new, make sure to go through your home and make sure that you don't already have something that will work for the same purpose.

Disposable Products

One of the worst things that's happened for the environment is something that makes life a little more convenient – disposable products. When you think about it, you can get almost everything in a disposable version such as:

- Diapers
- Eating utensils
- Cups
- Plates
- Napkins

- Cameras
- Razors
- Towels
- Sanitary products
- Makeup applicators
- Cat litter boxes
- Coffee filters
- Bottled water
- Air filters
- Sandwich bags (and other packaging)
- Paper bags
- Baby wipes
- And the list could go on and on…

For every item on the list – and hundreds of others – there's another option that's friendlier for the environment. While disposable items are convenient, they require a lot of energy to produce and they end up polluting the environment.

While you may not choose to ditch all of your disposable products, you might consider trading them out for permanent alternatives or items at least made from recycled or renewable resources. This is one of the most impactful changes you can make.

Reuse

Before you head to the trash can with an item, think about whether that's really the best place for it. There are many items that can be reused and repurposed rather than discarded. This can make a big difference in how much impact you have on the environment.

For example, instead of throwing away the plastic bags that come from the grocery store find a different use for them. They make great trash can liners, containers for cleaning out the litter box, and can be reused for carrying groceries another time.

Better yet, use bags that aren't designed to be thrown away. It's becoming more and more popular to by reusable shopping bags for groceries and other items. You can use them over and over again and can save hundreds of bags from a final resting place in the landfill.

Furniture is another item that can be reused instead of discarded. Even items that are dated can be updated instead of thrown away. A coat of paint, updated hardware, and polishing can help to restore an item's usefulness to you.

Updating an outfit with a modern accessory or tailoring can make it fresh and trendy again. Many people throw away clothing that could be salvaged with just a little bit of effort and a little know-how.

Instead of using those disposable items, work to use items that can be used over and over. For example, instead of using paper plates use real dishes that can be washed. Instead of disposable coffee filters, buy a permanent filter than can be washed and reused.

This may not seem like a big deal, but many small changes put together can have a big impact on the environment. Take a look at some options for reusing items instead of disposing of them:

- Use permanent handled razors instead of disposables
- Use cloth diapers that can be washed and reused
- Use feminine products that can be washed and reused
- Recover furniture when the pattern goes out of style
- Repaint cabinets and update hardware instead of buying new
- Move furniture from one part of the house to another room to give it a fresh look
- Use glass storage containers instead of disposable packaging
- Use a pitcher with a filter instead of bottled water
- Use washcloths instead of baby wipes

It's best to replace all disposable items with those that can be reused. However, not every person is ready to stop relying on disposable products altogether. You can make a difference by reducing your dependence on these items even if you don't quit using them altogether.

Evaluate the disposable products that you use and determine what items you can't live without and what items you can replace with reusable ones. This is a simple step but provides, perhaps, the greatest impact.

Items such as clothing that is badly stained or has holes can be given new life as towels or dust cloths. A piece of furniture that is broken can be transformed into a different type of decorative piece. You can breathe new life into everyday items with a little imagination and elbow grease.

Recycle

Recycling has become easier to do in recent years. As people have become aware of the problem with using up nonrenewable resources, systems have been put in place for recycling items you can no longer use.

Items made of paper and plastic are the most commonly recycled. Glass is also a material that can be readily recycled. If you live in an urban area, you may have curbside recycling available. This makes it convenient to recycle without having to go anywhere.

If you don't have recycling available at home, you may have to take your items to a recycling center. Luckily there are many places where you can go to recycle items in a convenient manner.

Many items can be recycled such as:

- Pizza boxes
- Water bottles
- Glass beer and wine bottles
- Paper
- Cardboard boxes
- Milk jugs and cartons
- Aluminum cans
- Grocery sacks (paper and plastic)
- Aluminum foil
- Soda bottles
- Shampoo bottles
- Lotion bottles

Plastic items have recycling numbers on the bottom of their containers. This helps you to understand which items can be recycled and which ones will not be accepted by recycling centers. Here's a look at which numbers are generally accepted:

- 1 and 2 are almost always accepted by recycling programs
- 3. 6, and 7 are generally not accepted
- 4 and 5 are sometimes accepted, but you'll need to ask the program

When you are part of a recycling program, they will generally give you information about what can and cannot be accepted. There are some things that might be accepted, but only under certain conditions.

For example, water bottles are recyclable but their lids are not. Some programs will take them with the lids, but others require you to do the work of removing them. Make sure to follow the guidelines set up by your program.

You should also consider natural recycling by using compost. This was discussed in Chapter 3. Composting can help you to save your kitchen waste from the landfill where it will rot and go unused.

When it comes to recycling, you're more likely to do it if it's convenient for you. You'll want to set up a system that makes it easy and part of your daily routine. For example, have several containers available in your kitchen. You'll want to have containers for:

- Trash
- Recycling
- Compost

If your recycling center requires you to sort your recycling, you'll also want to have containers for:

- Glass
- Plastic
- Paper/cardboard
- Aluminum

By sorting it immediately after use you'll save time later. It's also less messy to clean items and put them right into the recycling container. When it's time to take your items to the recycling center, it won't take much effort to pack them up and move them out.

Electronics Recycling

When it comes to electronics, there are some special considerations you need to make. Many electronics have heavy metals in them that need to be removed before they're disposed of. They also have parts that can be recycled.

Some retail locations, such as Target, provide recycling drop off centers. For example, you can drop off your cell phone in a special bin where it will be taken to recycling. You can also look online for cell phone recycling services that actually benefit charities.

Computers are more difficult to recycle and many donation centers won't accept them. Call ahead to see if a thrift store will take your electronics. If not, they can point you to a local place where you can have your materials recycled. Some places charge a fee for this service.

When All Else Fails…Donate

If you have items in your home that you simply can't use but are still in usable condition, try donating them. You can donate all kinds of items to local charities including:

· Furniture

· Clothing

· Baby items

· Toys

· Books

· Cd's

· Appliances

· Cookware

· Dishes

· Vases

· Decorative items

· Jewelry

· Automobiles

· Electronics

Not only will you give these items a chance for a new home, you'll be able to benefit a local charity. Look for a cause that you can really believe in. Local thrift shops benefit causes such as domestic abuse shelter and prevention, disease prevention, homeless shelters, and food pantries.

You may also want to consider getting rid of items using online lists such as Craigslist. You can give items away for free or even try to make a little money for them. Either way, you're benefiting the environment by keeping items out of the landfill.

You may think that nobody would want some of your old items, but you'd be surprised what someone else may think about your "junk". The saying, "one man's trash is another man's treasure," is absolutely true.

Keeping Earth Clutter Free

One of the greatest threats to the planet's health is waste and trash. Landfills are getting full and in the United States, trash is often collected and taken by barge to other countries. It's critical for the health of our planet that we manage how much we are using and throwing away.

Taking steps to reduce what you buy, reuse what you have, and recycle as many other items as possible is one of the most important things you can do as a citizen of Earth. It may take a lifestyle change, but these practices can become routine.

You'll find that limiting your consumption can also make you feel free from clutter. Many people collect items and all that clutter can make you feel disorganized and can make it difficult to keep things clean.

You can also save a lot of money when you take a break from consuming new items and look for ways to reuse items. That money can be used to get or stay out of debt, pay for future education expenses, or purchase more environmentally friendly items. Not only can you help to save the planet, you can also rescue your bank account.

Getting Rid of Toxic Waste: Keeping Poisons Out of the Landfill

Some items require special consideration when it comes to keeping the planet safe. While we can't totally end our dependence on these things, we can make sure that they're disposed of properly.

Items that fall into this category include:

- Paints
- Solvents
- Used batteries
- Motor oil

These items should not be thrown away in the trash or flushed down drains. Their effects can be dangerous to the environment and people. Most cities have places where you can take hazardous wastes to be disposed of properly.

Centers usually take items such as paint and solvents as well as batteries. When it comes to waste from working on vehicles, auto parts stores often provide services for recycling fluids. For example, you can take used motor oil to these stores.

If you don't have a local center for disposal, look for one in the nearest city or town. Many smaller towns have arrangements to share these facilities. Some larger cities will accept hazardous materials from other towns for a small fee.

A quick online search can help you find the closest, most convenient place to dispose of hazardous materials. While it may not be easy to dispose of this waste, it's worth the effort to keep the planet healthy.

Medications

Another threat to landfills as well as waterways is disposal of medications. Medications are frequently flushed down the toilet when they're no longer needed. However, this is bad for the water supply.

If you have a supply of medications that you no longer need, you should talk to your local pharmacist about proper disposal. Some pharmacies will allow you to drop off unused medications and they will handle disposal.

The Drug Enforcement Agency (DEA) also sets up programs around the country in the United States for proper disposal of prescription medications. Not only will this keep the environment safer, it could keep your family safer.

Particularly for families of teens, it's not a good idea to keep a supply of leftover medications in the home. Drugs such as muscle relaxers and narcotics should not be easily accessible to children who may not understand the consequences of using them.

Making It Easy on Yourself

Many sustainable living practices are a matter of making new habits and making things convenient. Dealing with hazardous materials can be easier if you have a system in place in your home for dealing with them.

For example, choose a safe place in your home where hazardous materials can be stored until you're able to dispose of them. Keep like items together. For example, have a container for storing batters, one for storing paints, etc.

Choose a regular time to take hazardous materials to the proper disposal center. For example, you could take paints and batteries two or three times yearly. You can also make sure to check your medicine cabinet twice yearly for excess and expired medications.

Part of keeping the planet healthy and keep your home healthy is minimizing the hazardous materials you use in the first place. By making as many choices as you can of non-toxic materials, you can limit the number of hazardous materials of which you need to dispose.

Fun for the Whole Family: Getting Kids Involved with Your New Lifestyle

Protecting the planet is important for you. In order to make sure you instill the same values in your children, you'll need to get them involved in the process. There are many benefits to getting the whole family to participate.

Why Kids Should Get Involved

There are many reasons why kids benefit from practicing sustainable living. If you're interested in making the planet healthier for your kids, you'll want them to continue those practices as they grow older.

Kids who participate in sustainable living are:

- more likely to learn gardening skills and eat vegetables
- more likely to continue recycling as they become adults
- physically healthier
- more conscious of ethical treatment of animals
- less concerned with material possessions

Not only will your children benefit from sustainable living, they can take over some of the responsibilities – and that benefits you! There are some really fun ways to get your kids involved in this type of lifestyle. When you make it fun for them, they'll be happy to help.

Making Sustainable Living Fun

If you're trying to help kids understand the importance of sustainable living, it helps to get them to participate in the process. Here are a few tips for getting kids involved in your new lifestyle:

· get kids to help plant vegetables and fruits in the garden – there are many interesting varieties that are fun for kids

· set up recycling centers in your home with pictures on the containers for kids who can't read yet

· involve children in the process of painting and repurposing furniture items

· give your children chores to help take care of agricultural animals on your property

· teach children to sew

· teach children to cook with fresh vegetables and fruits

· have family nights when you discuss the importance of the planet

· plant trees together in your backyard that produce fruit and flowers

· take children with you to thrift stores and teach them how to make choices about what is appropriate for use

· volunteer with your children – help them to see that the choices they are making can impact others in a good way

· let your children take part in the planning process of gardening or farming, give them a role and responsibilities

· read children's stories about the earth and the environment

Involving your children it making changes to your home that promote sustainable living can help them to develop habits that will last a lifetime. Your children will be the future generation that will continue to care for the planet.

Kids may not always want to participate, but by making it a fun adventure and giving them a part to play, they'll be more likely to enjoy it. Realize that they may have times when they don't want to accept restrictions.

It's important to help children understand the purpose of the procedures you're putting in place. Most kids feel happy and excited when they are doing something good for others. Help them to understand how sustainable living is beneficial to other people as well as themselves.

Sustainable Living Tips: Small Choices that Make a Big Impact

If you're not ready to make huge changes, you may feel better just taking a few small steps. There are several simple, quick things you can do that will make an immediate impact on the earth. In this chapter you'll learn some simple steps.

You can practice one of these changes or all of them. Even making one change can have a big impact on the environment. Don't just throw out the whole idea of sustainable living because it seems like a major lifestyle overhaul.

Instead, focus on making small changes one at a time. Once you've instituted one habit, you can add another and another if you choose. If not, at least you've done something to benefit the planet.

- Plant a tree in your yard
- Purchase a pitcher water filtering system instead of purchasing bottled water
- Grow an herb garden on your back porch
- Buy vegetables from local farmers
- Look for organic produce in your local supermarket
- Use natural cleaners such as vinegar to mop the floor instead of toxic chemicals
- Update a piece of furniture instead of throwing it away
- Give away or donate clothes that no longer fit
- Switch to fluorescent light bulbs
- Start recycling paper instead of throwing it away
- Organize a recycling center in your home for glass, plastic, and paper
- Use motion sensors for lighting fixtures to save energy

- Find an energy company that locally provides energy from windmills
- Recycle cans
- Buy reusable shopping bags instead of using paper or plastic
- Use plastic grocery sacks as trash can liners or reuse them for groceries
- Use renewable resources when remodeling your home – such as bamboo wood for flooring
- Buy items made from recycled materials
- Take old medications back to the pharmacy instead of throwing them away
- Turn your thermostat up a few degrees in summer and down a few degrees in winter
- Cover your windows with thermal curtains
- Make use of natural light instead of using electricity during the day
- Walk to the store instead of driving
- Take the bus instead of driving to work each day
- Set up a carpool to go to school or work
- Purchase a car with high gas mileage
- Choose one day a week to skip eating meat
- Make meat a side dish rather than the main meal each night

Any one of these choices can help to protect the planet. Doing something – even if it's small- is better than doing nothing to conserve Earth's resources. With every positive change you make, you're working toward making the planet healthier and preserving it for future generations.

If you're not ready to overhaul your whole lifestyle, taking it one step at a time can be beneficial. In the next chapter we'll look at how to make a plan for a more sustainable future for you and your family.

Taking the First Steps Toward a Fresh Way of Life: Making a Plan and Getting Started

When it comes to sustainable living, you may find that it helps to make a plan for changing your lifestyle. You may be satisfied with choosing a few simple tips that can make the planet a little healthier, but for some people that's not enough.

Set a Goal

Before you get started, make a goal for sustainable living. Do you want to save money? Do you want to grow your own food? Do you see yourself practicing sustainable living in an urban area? Or do you envision living on a self-sustaining property growing your own food and raising livestock?

Make sure you understand what you envision for the future and take steps to reaching that goal. For some sustainable living goals will take more time than for others. Make sure to set goals that are appropriate for where you are in your life right now.

Making a Plan

After you've set a goal, it's time to create a plan. Begin by looking at where you'd like to end. If you'd like to be self-sustaining within five years, what do you need to do each year to prepare for that goal?

Decide what steps you will take and when. It may help to use a calendar or make a vision board of what you'd like to achieve. These can serve as reminders for your ultimate sustainable living goals.

Most importantly, don't become discouraged. When you're making changes in your lifestyle, you're bound to have some setbacks. Don't let those setbacks keep you from realizing your final goals. Do the best you can and accept that it won't be perfect.

While you want to make sure the planet gets protected as much as possible, you need to remember that even small changes have big impact. You'll be helping to secure the future of the planet with every good choice you make.